Brooklyn & Queens Transit Corporation
Brooklyn, N. Y.
TOTAL NUMBER OF P.C.C. CARS OPERATED 100 (January 1936)

The following information covers
ONE HUNDRED P.C.C. CARS

Built by St. Louis Car Co.   Equipped by General Electric

Weight for car equipped (without load): 33,360 lb
Seating capacity: 59
Weight per passenger seat: 566 lb
Length over bumpers: 46 ft, 0 in.
Overall width (at window sill): 8 ft, 3⅝ in.
Width of aisle: 23½ in.
Width of seat: 33 in.
Single- or double-end operation: single-end
Truck centers: 22 ft, 6 in.
Wheel base: 6 ft, 0 in.
Track gauge: 4 ft, 8½ in.
Type of truck: P.C.C. design built by Clark Equipment Co.
Wheel diameter: 25 in.
Number and type of motors: four General Electric Type GE-1198
                                              (one)

One of the major contributions in the evolution and preservation of the trolley industry was the Brooklyn & Queens Transit Corporation (B&QT) faithful pioneers of the Electric Railroader's President Conference Committee's (ERPCC) car, the PCC. Brooklyn never lost its commitment to the ERPCC and its goals. Both the Depression and the private automobile ownership rolled on, causing other companys to quit the committee. Through the Depression, the B&QT continued its faith with the project. The B&QT would be the first transit company to order a 101 cars. One car in this order would go to Boston and another to Pittsburgh. In 1936 the B&QT ordered 99 St Louis built PCC cars and one Clark built car replacing the Pittsburgh car. This fleet would end all trolley operations in Brooklyn in 1956.

This small work is dedicated to each PCC in the Brooklyn fleet. Since this was a small fleet, each car is represented in some form with its operational history during its reign. As time passes an increasing majority of our population has never seen, let alone ridden, a Brooklyn trolley. This is a land that used to be known as the city inhabited by trolley dodgers. Now, like the baseball team, we can bring the Borough back to the decades from 1936 to 1956.

There are a number of books out on the technical achievements of the PCC. My goal is to give a reality to the existence of one type of trolley car. Everyday they went forth in all weather in many areas of Brooklyn and interacted with the people and the neighborhoods. They were a great part of the life and culture of one of the most gifted and important areas of America, Brooklyn. It became clear that the PCC succeeded in overcoming many operational problems as the B&QT and other PCC companies compared notes with the ERPCC. It was an historical and very successful collaboration between the designers and the users. Never in public transportation history has there been any coalition with such a successful result, that is still felt to this day. The PCC is pure American original.

The B&QT proved that new cars could improve the ridership on the lines that they served. They wou[...] [...]ons enabling fewer cars on one line. The continuing reports issued from the B&QT must have had an impression on other [...] ent company BMT) was one of the most respected properties in the nation. If you look at the time during the Dep[...] ordering trolley and rapid transit equipment that was very innovative and distinctive in comparison to other cor[...] success everywhere except in the New York political arena. The impending purchase by the City government forc[...] relations fight to extol the good sense of electric traction and how to build on past success and translate that into the City's future opera[...] It was a battle they would lose. In a tribute to the company and the cars, I bring out some of these interesting facts.

A work called "A STUDY OF THE ADVANTAGES OF MODERN ELECTRIC VEHICLES FOR MODERNIZING SURFACE MASS TRANSPORTATION IN BROOKLYN" by Vice President and General Manager of the B&QT, William Rossell. The purpose of the work was to show that Brooklyn had a great investment in electric public transportation and it is one that would pay off in the future. The B&QT reported ridership up 33% when PCC cars were employed. They showed that when the riding public took a vote for modern trolley service over bus service, the trolley cars won and won big. In Chicago, of 2546 votes, 2155 voted for the trolley. In Cleveland, 2294 votes, 2350 voted for trolley service. In Brooklyn it was 1061 out of 1400 votes for trolley service.

The B&QT went on to point out the cost of converting to bus which, at that time, was a gasoline powered bus. The figures were based on total annual operating expenses, excluding general tax, gas tax, and depreciation and interest on present investment.

59-Pass. Trolley	45-Pass. Gas Bus	35-Pass. Gas Bus	25-Pas Gas Bus
$8,557,252	**$10,033,931**	**$12.063,156**	**$15,659,454**
Requires 765	Requires 1114	Requires 1434	Requires 2007

These figures were based on Brooklyn having 28 trolley lines and the fleet required to cover the ridership derived from these lines. It would be 179 miles of track that included: Flatbush, Smith/Coney Island, Utica/Reid, Fifth, DeKalb, Nostrand, Mc Donald/Vanderbilt, Metropolitan, Gravesend/Church, Crosstown, Tompkins, Flushing/Ridgewood, Ralph/Rockaway, Wilson, Richmond Hill, Putnam, Flushing, Nostrand Shuttle, Erie Basin, St Johns Pl., Ocean, Gates, Church, Graham, Fulton, Lorimer, Seventh and Notons Point.

Twelve lines were to be converted to trackless trolley lines and they were: Hamilton-Bay Ridge, Grand St., Bergen St., Jamaica Ave., Franklin, Myrtle-Court, Third, Sumner-Sackett, Ralph, Eighth, Sea Gate and Fifteenth Street. The fleet would consist of 207 Coaches on 73 route miles. The B&QT pointed out that electric vehicles did not lose their performance characteristics with age. As a result, transit companies were depreciating modern trolley equipment on a 15-20 year basis and electric bus on a 10-15 year basis as compared with 6-8 years for gas buses. In addition the commitment in facilities that maintained a vast trolley and electric bus fleet already existed. It was pointed out that operating trolleys and trolley coaches were easier for the operator and better for the operators dealing with auto traffic.

This report went on to document other features of this proposal. If one used common sense, this would be the policy that should have been carried out, but this was not meant to be. The City, when it took over operations did eventually convert 6 lines to trolley coach operations, But never purchased more PCC cars. The report was correct for the Brooklyn PCC cars. They retired after 20 years in operation. In 1960 when all trolley coach operations ended, the trolley coach fleet was 12 years in operation. When politics manages transit, common sense and doing the right thing means nothing.

1000

A unique relationship developed over a period of years with the Clark Equipment Company of Battle Creek, Michigan and the BMT management. This relationship would bring the non-car building company into the car building business. It would start with the order for one PCC car. Clark Equipment was the only manufacturer of PCC B-2 trucks for St. Louis and Pullman Standard. It had participated as a manufacturing company in the work of the ERPCC committee. Perhaps during this time Clark and the BMT developed a working relationship of persons with similar goals which evolved into products that would effect the future of rapid transit.

The firm must have sensed a market for fleets of cars and the B&QT needed one car to replace the one car that went to Pittsburgh, so #1000 was produced. The car was delivered shortly after the cars were coming off the line at St. Louis Car Company. It was much more boxy in shape than the St. Louis design but more stylish when compared to the Brilliner's being sold by J G Brill. The new features over the St. Louis design were the use of aluminum construction , standee windows, and a few mechanical changes. Other than that, it was essentially the same. The Clark car was never made an odd ball orphan like the PCC model A or B would become. These two experimental cars, the first built by Twin Coach and the second by Pullman were scrapped by B&QT in 1938.

The front and rear ends of 1000 were altered after several accidents in 1946. From this point on it was nicked named the "Frankenstein monster" by crews and fans. The car stayed with her St Louis companions to the end of street car service in 1956. Clark would go on to build the articulated compartment cars called the "Blue Birds" for the elevated and subway lines of the BMT. One demo unit was built and later an order for fifty such units was to be built. When City management took over only five had been built. The city would cancel the rest of the order. These units were the first to incorporate the advances of PCC mechanical equipment in a rapid transit car. No other public transit equipment was produced by Clark.

1000

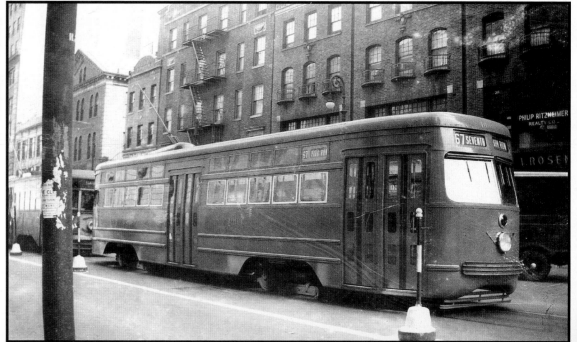

(top) The new kid on the block running on the Seventh Avenue line, moving down Seventh Avenue with other traffic of the period. (right) The Clark car is pictured on Flatbush near Dean Street in May 1938. A seven year old 6000 series single ended Peter Witt car on Flatbush Avenue route is behind. Two hundred of those were ordered in the depression from Brill and Osgood Bradley. (middle) In 1947 at Ebbets Field 1000 displays the different look the car acquired after having its lower sash rebuilt.

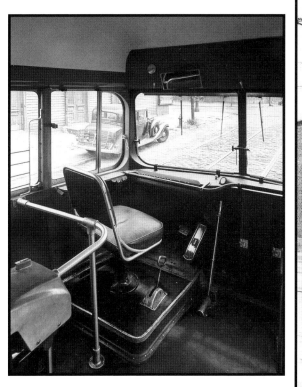

1001

(top) 1001 is at DeKalb shop complex undergoing testing by the General Electric Company. It has not yet gone into revenue service. The test cables to monitor on board performance can be seen coming out of the open windows. These were to monitor the front and rear trucks, motors and controller. The B&QT would participate with other cities to iron the flaws out of this revolutionary vehicle during BMT ownership and into City ownership. This constant correspondence with the ERPCC members would bring many changes mechanically and cosmetically to the fleets of PCC cars in the future. (top left) The operators seat is a neat simple arrangement. This car is controlled by two foot pedals to start and stop the car. The control and brake handles are gone. All the switches to control doors and lights etc., are arranged in front of the operators hand bar. (bottom left) PCC also brought attention to a car's interior decor.

5

1001

(top) 1001 has just picked up a passenger and turns on to Neptune Avenue on a Sunday morning in Coney Island. It only has a few more months to do this service. The year is 1956. (right) 9th Avenue & 20th Street Barn kept 1001 and its companions repaired and sheltered. It was also a lab facility for the ERPCC equipment tests.

1002

Our subject is just coming down off the Brooklyn Bridge while operating on the McDonald/Vanderbilt route in 1948. The trolley now occupies what used to be the El tracks. The vacated former trolley tracks can still be seen on the bridge roadway. In 1883 when the Brooklyn Bridge opened it pioneered a very successful cable railway. Today no public transportation of any variety crosses the great bridge.

1003

(left) 1003 was the first PCC to get the green and silver paint scheme of the Board of Transportation and went on a photo opportunity. 1003 is about to move on to the Brooklyn Bridge from Park Row. The year is 1946 and it has taken six years since the City took over the B&QT to pick a corporate color scheme. Several variations of the brownish gray B&QT scheme were tried with other additional color touches. (bottom left) The interior of 1003 shows the nickel turnstile right at the head of the photograph; the car is a decade old. In 1955 a fire broke out at 9th Avenue & 20th Street Barn with 1003 as one of victims. Here it is being towed away to the scrap yard. In a year the rest of the PCC will follow 1003.

1004

(top) The riders on the Smith Street line are the recipients of the new PCC cars. Pictured above, 1004 is running on Smith Street at Bergen Street in 1946. This early PCC design allowed the front windshields to open for ventilation and it's being tried on this summer's day. (right) What a simply beautiful object the PCC is. This photograph of 1004 shows off the lines and shape of this transportation object perfectly. Keats stated "A thing of beauty is a joy forever." I think this shot bears the poet out. Brooklyn did well by being faithful to the development of this important transportation vehicle.

1005

In ten years of service the front dash has gotten a few dents. The steel panels of the PCC were a lot thinner than other cars in the Brooklyn fleet. This will be a continuing theme in the PCC fleet's whole operating life. The anti climber will get bigger to meet the constant challenge. Each year traffic in the Borough will only get worse for trolley service. Passenger islands will eventually get in the way of automobile traffic and will have to go. In 1947 Livington Street still has trolley stop islands in the roadway. 1005 is on the Seventh Avenue line.

1006

Our car is leaving the former 39th Street Ferry Loop in Sunset Park and turning on to Second Avenue. Long ago steam trains took bathers from the ferry and steam-ships to Coney Island. If we look straight ahead, we see the South Brooklyn Railway yards and right of way that now supports the BMT subway lines. Once the former 39th Street Terminal stood in that yard. It was never used as a terminal but converted into a major over haul shop for both rapid and trolley fleets. The year is 1956 and the last year that public rail transit will run to this area.

1007

1007 leads a line of other PCC cars across 13th Avenue between 39th & 38th Streets, a very busy shopping street for this area of Brooklyn . The Culver El now ends at Ditmas Avenue. Today both the trolley service and El operation and structure are gone from this neighborhood. Today houses have been built on the Culver rights of way.

1008

Rerouted on Route 72/Smith Street 1008 is turning from Adams Street on to Joralemon Street on a summer June day in 1947. Downtown Brooklyn is the big city that was the center and beginning of Brooklyn when it was itself, a city. It still feels that way.

1009

It is a great moment for the B&QT on October 1, 1936. Mayor LaGuardia cuts the ribbon at Park Row Terminal to inaugurate PCC trolley service for Brooklyn. 1009 and other cars will carry the special guests to downtown Brooklyn. Here he is introducing a truly streamlined and sophisticated modern streetcar to the streets of his city, but it would be the bus that he would envision in his future city. The man to his far left is Mr. William Menden of the Brooklyn Manhattan Transit Company. In his mind, the PCC was the new age of better transportation and the culmination of a lot of hard work. The company will spend the next few years before being purchased by the City to try to change His Honors mind about trolley cars and their Brooklyn system. The mayor will in the end win out over minds like Menden. (bottom) Years later the two great enemies of trolley operation are apparent behind 1009 as it is about to pull into the West 5th Street Terminal in Coney Island in her last year of operation.

1010

(right) The PCC was still being tested and changed while they ran the streets of Brooklyn. 1010 would support a test that made it a little different than the others. In 1939 1010 was fitted with a new front ventilator similar to the GM bus design of the time. It was hoped that it would improve air circulation, but 1010 would be the only PCC altered in this way. 1010 was easy to pick out of the fleet because of this installation. (top) 1010 runs through the slush that a few days ago was a big snow storm. It would be the Brooklyn fleet's last snow storm. The year is 1956 on the route 35/Church Avenue.

1011

Here 1011 turns off Church Avenue on to 37th Street to parallel the right of way of the South Brooklyn Railway and the Culver El in the last year of operation. The building behind is part of the former 37th Street car barn of the Nassau Electric that was merged into the BRT system. 1011 in its career helped test "All Electric" equipment. Today there is nothing that remains of traction history in this neighborhood.

1012

Here 1012 is pictured in December 1942 in the DeKalb shop's front yard. The car is high because it is mounted on special shop trucks that the DeKalb shops used when cars were in for an overhaul. It is correctly signed for a line that will never operate PCC cars. Compare this photo with the one on the right and you will see the changes made on the front skirting under the anti-climber. In 1941 it is original but in 1946 it is cut open exposing the tow bar hook. It becomes less and less streamlined as it moves through the years. (right) On a 1946 fan trip, 1012 is coming from the back yard at Fresh Pond depot. Fan trips took a PCC where they never ran. Fresh Pond had every type of Brooklyn trolley equipment except PCC's. The car is painted in one of the experimental color schemes that the City tried. Yellow stripping along the belt rail was added to the full grey-brown color and bright red scheme.

1013

(left) 1013 is operating on route 63/Coney Island Avenue. It is headed for the West 5th Street Terminal. The old Sea Breeze Hotel is a last reminder of the resort area that was Coney Island. At one time, the area was dotted with little and big hotels and many a wonderful summer was had by the millions. But now times and travel change things for the public is driving to Jones Beach and other resorts just a drive away. (below) In 1955, 1013 ducks under Ocean Parkway on Church Avenue, toward McDonald Avenue which is another advantage the trolley had over a bus. Upon abandonment of trolley service, this underpass will be covered over but the rails will be sent to the Bradford trolley museum where Brooklyn cars can run over Brooklyn rails once more.

1014

1014 is operating on the 69/McDonald-Vanderbilt line in the summer of 1945. The war is over and it is back to basics. Here our car stops for one of the traffic lights of that period at DeKalb Avenue with 1007 coming up behind. It will cross the DeKalb Avenue line that was started by the Brooklyn City and Newtown Railroad; Vanderbilt line was started by Nassau Electric Railroad. (bottom) Ten years later and it is running in Brighton Beach area; this area is a little quieter in the winter time. However the locals are still providing ridership. 1014 is on Coney Island Avenue line at Brighton Beach Avenue. In the back ground is Mrs Stahl's, selling a mainstay of the local diet- "a true Brooklyn soul food, knishes". It still in business at this printing.

1015

With its front window open, 1015 moves down Prospect Park West. Here the trolley tracks were on one side of the street along the great Prospect Park. The warm breeze and beautiful park made one feel, if only for a few blocks, as if you were in the country. The PCC design is a stark contrast to the 1941 Twin Coach bus in the far left operating the Hamilton Avenue route on 16th Street/Erie Basin route in 1945.

1016

It is the first day of PCC car service in Brooklyn. Here 1016 is about to cross the Brooklyn Bridge perhaps for the first time. The Park Row El Terminal can be seen in the background. This is the only place were PCC's will run in the Borough of Manhattan. From the auto and truck traffic of the day, one can see what a giant step the PCC car design was. From its headlight to trolley retriever, the PCC was a powerful design. (top) In 1968 1016 was taken from the scrap yard where it sat since 1956 and moved to Richmond town in Staten Island. It was part of an attempt to try and save another PCC car. Sadly it failed and 1016 was destroyed.

1017

Our car made it is far as Cortelyou Road in the blizzard. Not even the cover of the Culver El has helped 1017 in the big blizzard of 1947 . Some of the switches leading to the South Brooklyn Railway and 36th Street yard have been uncovered but there is still a lot to do. The date is December 29th and, even three days after the storm, all over Brooklyn most of the trolley equipment was still frozen in position, . The storm intensified as the PM rush hour was under way and a lot of cars were out on their lines. This prevented the snow plows and sweepers from doing their work and 1017 became stuck with the rest of the Brooklyn fleet.

1018

(left) An Oldsmobile crosses the Bergen Street intersection with 1018 on Vanderbilt Avenue in 1949. The electric bus wires of the Bergen Street line can be seen overhead. Brooklyn had a candy store, drug store and bar on almost every block. Each neighborhood was an independent area, with its own vendors servicing that neighborhood. Sometimes an outstanding butcher or baker would have housewife's include a trolley trip to another neighborhood to complete their shopping. Brooklynites were not discouraged by trolley travel; they relied on it. Its dependable service made Brooklynites a very mobile society. (bottom) Here in late 1941 track work was being done on Livingston Street and 1018 is rerouted on Myrtle Avenue on a block that does not exist today. It has just passed under the Adams Street station. The station is perched over the street intersection but the tracks turn up Myrtle headed north from Adams to Sands Street Station. This strange layout was used because Adams Street was too narrow to include the building.

1019

A woman has just gotten off one of those new trolley cars. The new cars are holding down 68/Smith-Coney Island near 9th Avenue on October 19, 1936. The riders inside the new car are astonished by this new trolley and from the clean windows and shiny chrome, who wouldn't be? A lot of other trolley executives will travel to take a look at these new cars and in turn, order some for their cities. The B&QT work has paid off. In a line from the poet, Vachel Lindsay " Once they had a vision, then they had religion".

1020

1020 has just crossed Second Avenue from the private right of way to the old 39th Street Ferry Terminus in 1953. It must be a Sunday for all the factories in this Bush Terminal area are quiet. No trucks are rumbling by; just the quiet operation of a lone and empty PCC car. (bottom) A view from a roof of the Beverly Tavern at the intersection of Church and McDonald Avenues. 1020 takes on passengers in the last year of operation. A famous bakery, Ebingers, is right next to the Beverly Theater. They too will pass from Brooklyn and will also be mourned. If you ever tasted their baked goods, nothing else has to be said.

1021

1021 to the left, is joined by 1037 and 1079 in 1941 at the old Coney Island & Brooklyn depot at W.5th Street. Coney Island still offered an escape from the realities of a Brooklyn at war. All three cars show the dents that a daily battle with traffic in Brooklyn streets do to the front dash of a PCC. I don't recall any other city that had such a problem, perhaps Pittsburgh? (left) It is 1956 and 1021 tows another PCC down McDonald Avenue for the last time. They are headed to Avenue X and Coney Island yards where they will be dismantled.

1022

During the summer of 1946, 1022, seen here under the Brooklyn approach to the Manhattan Bridge, has just passed 6034 which is operating on the Flushing Avenue line. Ten years of service have shown little change to the car as it moves down Jay Street. (right) On Jay Street again but a year later in 1947. The blizzard will keep the cars on Jay Street for some days. The overpass was to the Myrtle El station at Jay Street. The Myrtle & Lexington Avenue lines were cut back to Jay Street after the Fulton El, Sands Street complex and Brooklyn Bridge service were abandoned.

1023

1023 on MacDonald Avenue at Avenue X under the Culver El. What is today an Avenue was originally the right of way of the South Brooklyn Railway and the Prospect Park & Coney Island Railroad. In time it was electrified and El and trolley cars ran together to New York's great seaside resort for every man. Eventually the rural countryside became populated with homes and apartment buildings and the trains had to be elevated. Later in 1954 the IND subway would complete the transformation. (bottom) 1023 is having a quiet moment in Grand Army Plaza in 1950. A GM bus can be seen to the far left. It is running on the now Union Street bus route. It was part of a fleet of 900 GM buses in 1948 with Mack providing another 600 in 1950-51. Brooklyn has been replacing these fleets every 13-16 years. A bus does not last as long as a trolley.

1024

Through private right of way the 69/McDonald - Vanderbilt Avenue line ran from Neptune Avenue to the West 5th Street terminal at Coney Island. Here, in the past, small buildings that were once small summer hotels and rentals later became homes or apartments. There tracks were once part of the Culver line that had a large wood terminal at Surf Avenue for El trains. A new PCC heads toward its present Coney Island Terminal in the bitter winter months of 1937. The power lines are from the small sub-station behind our car.

1025

1035 runs along the wall that covers the IND 6th Avenue subway elevation to the Culver El and the Ditmas Avenue station. This connection was opened on October 30, 1954. A shuttle would run from Ditmas Avenue behind to 9th Avenue and a connection to the West End line. This was made possible by the merger of the BMT and the Independent's system by the Board of Transportation. The lone trolley poles built into this wall can still be seen today. Even the Culver shuttle structure has been torn down.

1026

The PCC is on 15th Street headed for Erie Basin loop. With the war on and Brooklyn lined with docks and ship yards, the Brooklyn fleet carried workers to and from work during all shifts. The speed and efficiency of the PCC design helped. They came at the right time and added greatly to a taxed fleet. The PCC with all of its success would not see repeat orders like other cities after the war. The fault did not involve the car but involved politics. The politicians did not want reorders and instead they went for "clean gas buses". The B&QT won the battle but it lost the war. In little more than a decade after the war these clean buses were everywhere trolley lines used to be. (bottom) 1026 turns onto Neptune Avenue in the summer 1944. 2551 on Seagate waits for the newest step in trolley technology to move on. This picture also shows how far Brooklyn transportation has come. Near the end of the 19th Century this intersection saw steam excursion trains that would eventually lead to electric trolley and surface running el cars to Els that supported subway service into Manhattan. This is a busy spot and has been such for 100 years.

1027

The car has not arrived yet to Brooklyn rails but it is close, it is in Sunnyside yards of the Long Island Railroad in Long Island City. The paper placard in the window states proudly "built by St Louis Car Co. St Louis". These same placards will decades later be in windows of 100's of R-Type subway cars made for the New York City Transit Authority by the St Louis firm.

1028

Well, on the streets of Brooklyn anything can happen or not happen. Here 1028's being towed back to Dekalb Shop via Canarsie Depot. It broke down on the line and a tow car had to be called. The year is 1943 and the wrecker here is a 4500 series. The 4500's had been out of regular passenger service before the PCC's arrived.

1029

Brand new PCC fleet with its wax shine reflects the great structure. When PCCs were introduced on a line the ridership began to rise. The B&QT was proud to show that people would use public transit more when public transit was more attractive, efficient and comfortable. Most of the Brooklyn trolley riders sat on wooden seats, so the contoured leather seats of the PCC were a welcomed change. 1029 is headed to Park Row terminal in Manhattan. (below) With most of its windows open, it is the summer of 1941. 1019 cruises through the Park Slope area of Brooklyn, headed for Grand Army Plaza. It is passing Prospect Park West at 15th Street with the park on one side and an elegant apartment house on the other side of this avenue. The PCC cars, when compared to the other cars in the Brooklyn fleet, were quieter and less distracting to Brooklyn's more affluent residents.

1030

Here in Grand Army Plaza in January 1939, 1030 is negotiating a bad snow storm. The trolley system functioned very well in snow storms because by law, the traction companies had to clear their own lines with an army of snow plows and sweepers. Went they converted to buses this benefit was lost and added to the Department of Sanitation's burden.

1031

Crossing the busy junction at McDonald and Church Avenues. This would be the last stand for the once great B&QT trolley system. The 18 year old 1031 heads toward Coney Island Depot. The trolley has had some changes over the years. These can be seen mainly on the front dash. First the "Next Car" sign went, next a larger anti-climber was installed and eventually the chrome PCC headlight wings would disappear. The smooth ride did not change with age, that remained the same. The Greater New York Savings bank is now Astoria Federal Savings Bank.

1032

1032 has just left the Canarsie Depot loop and is headed to First Avenue in Sunset Park. There are several stretches on Church Avenue that are busy shopping areas. This was where the speed of the line was often reduced to a crawl. The PCC was very suited for this type of service with its improved braking and acceleration. This enabled the car to inch along with the crawling auto traffic. In the window of the car are the notices that soon buses will be taking on this responsibility. The bus will not improve the speed or dependability. In fact, it will increase the running time.

1033/1034

Moving past the Sanders Theater, 1033 comes to a stop to pickup two passengers. Perhaps they are headed to Abraham & Strauss, Martins or Namm's and Loeser's departments stores. When you purchased clothes for a special occasion you went as they say, "Downtown," to shop. (right) 1034 leads a small parade of PCC cars down the underpass at Ocean Parkway. There must have been some line blockage. Now riders waiting at exposed trolley stations on this cold March 1952 day, in a number of minutes, will be treated to a flood of service.

1035

Here is a scene most enthusiasts never see-the interior and working of the shop forces. Perhaps for insurance reasons we have this image of 1035 in the DeKalb Shop. The front skirting has been replaced and spot painted. In the rear we can see another PCC and one of the big snow sweepers being repaired. The long pit tells us this was a big and busy facility. (right) 1035, along with a few other PCC cars were rescued for a while by being used in a boy's day camp at Far Rockaway.

1036

After the war, year by year, there will be fewer and fewer automobile parking spots. An operation such as both tracks on one side of the street, as pictured here, would interfere with the steady stream of traffic. Even with the collusion of the auto lobby to destroy the street railway business, it was still American's love of the auto that buried the street railway industry. The majority of new light rail lines today stay clear of sharing right of way with the auto. In today's world, it's slow moving congested traffic, not slow moving streetcars, that are to be dreaded. The trolley in a number of areas had a private right of way that would not be inherited by the bus. Here we see an example as 1036 speeds down Prospect Park West in 1944. (bottom) 1036 unfortunately has derailed just before turning into the West 5th Street terminal. A helpless 1003 and 1035 along with 1036 have just let off their passengers, who are looking over the problem. The curved trolley poles at the rear of the depot were made that way for clearance for a former amusement ride. Perhaps a good citizen has gotten something out of the trunk to get the car back on the tracks. The date of this mishap is May 30, 1940. Perhaps some riders feel they should have gone to the World's Fair instead of Coney Island.

1037

This is how the entrance on the Brooklyn side to the Bridge looked in 1946. In 1944 the El trains were removed from the bridge. The large El Terminal of Sands Street, where all Brooklyn El lines converged with the trolley lines that went over the bridge, was gone. A large open space emerged. Now the street car occupied the center tracks where the El train and cable railway once ran. As the subways grew, the original, prime crossing of the Brooklyn Bridge grew less important. The original cable railway conceived by Roebling was at one time the shortest and busiest railway in New York State. It was a little over one mile. There is no evidence of any of these former activities today.

1038

It is a fan trip for the last day of trolley service on the Williamsburgh Bridge, December 4, 1948. The B&QT had what is today the eastbound inner roadway as a private right of way, just for trolley cars. It ran the length of the Williamsburgh Bridge. (top right) Here we see 1038 stopped at the Bedford/Driggs Avenue Station on the Brooklyn side of the Bridge. This was used by many factory workers in this area of Williamsbugh. The Manhattan end terminated in several loops parallel to the Jamaica El's subway station. (top left) 1038 is pictured at the Delancey Street subway station loop. Many Brooklynites would go into Manhattan for the bargains they could find on Delancey and the other lower eastside shops. (bottom left) A photo stop at the foot of the Brooklyn side of the Bridge and its holding up 6044 behind. If they rushed, we would not have what's on this page. 1038 and 1067 were the last cars to wear the B&QT grey colors.

1039

1039 moves off the 16th Avenue loop and onto McDonald Avenue right of way. The dark burnt out building in the background is the remains of the Kensington Junction switch tower. It once controlled the connection of the Culver line El cars and a number of Brooklyn trolley lines when they were surface running and when hundreds of thousands of beach goers rode to Coney Island. Huge El trains shared the same track with 14 bench opens the whole length of the line to the Coney Island Terminal. This would be unthinkable today. Many of the beach goers took notice of the area between this junction and Coney Island and would decide to reside there. Stores, churches and temples would follow. Today subway trains running every three minutes in the rush hour are required to move the inhabitants.

1040

1040 moves up Church Avenue at E.10th Street a few days after a good snow storm. It was the last call for ancient snow sweepers and plows that did the job they were built for. The back of an old Checker cab moves past the PCC. This was a time when you could get a cab in this area of Brooklyn. The trolley line pole filial (center of picture) was a type used by the Nassau Electric Company and not the traditional derby hat of the Brooklyn Rapid transit company. Today, an old trolley pole is a rare sight.

1041

The car is about to cross over a draw bridge over the Gowanus Canal on 9th Street Draw bridge. Here barges carry a wide variety of goods into Brooklyn. The structure above is the Independent subway line.

1042

Being released from Dekalb shops for war duties. The waxed body days are over. It's small spot painting on the cars side panels now. During the war effort the top part of the head lamp is painted black, for less glare to be spotted by enemy planes. Soon a hostler will take 1042 back to 9th Avenue depot and bring back another PCC needy of shop work at DeKalb.

1043

On Neptune Avenue 1043 is about to turn on to the private right of way to the West 5th Street depot. In the July heat of 1954, some people still take the trolley to the amusements found at Coney Island. Subways took away the crowds that the trolley carried at one time .

1044

The last of the Birney fleet (7158,7122 & 7169) are waiting to be pulled apart in Coney Island on December 6, 1937. The Coney Island area near Avenue X, is where most of the souls departed from the Brooklyn fleet. The new hope for electric railway's is the shiny new PCC cars, not the small Birney safety cars. The BRT had high hopes for the Birney one-man safety cars. They purchased over two hundred of them. But in a few years they ran only on small shuttles and lightly used lines. Two lasted into the 1950's by being rebuilt as rail girders (one for the rapid transit system and one for the trolley system). Many would be sold to other cities and perhaps one of the ex-Brooklyn fleet may show up again.

1045

Coney Island Avenue provided a wide boulevard for the PCC cars. There were marked passenger islands in the roadway and plenty of room for the auto traffic. When a PCC was approaching blocks away, you could hear the humming in the overhead wire. Here 1045 is about to pass over another PCC line at Church Avenue in 1954. McDonald Avenue and Coney Island Avenue line ended at the same depot at West 5th Street . The streets in this southern part of Brooklyn that run north and south are wider and straighter. Coney Island Avenue from Prospect Park runs as straight as an arrow to the ocean.

1046

The car is about to pass the Flatbush Avenue Terminal of the Long Island Railroad. The Fifth Avenue El is gone so you now can see the terminal. Many passengers of the Long Island Railroad would change to the trolley for destinations further into downtown Brooklyn. We can see part of the Williamsburgh Savings Bank Building with the largest built-in clock tower in the world. The Brooklyn Academy of Music is near by.

1047

Coming down to the home stretch and about to cross over into Coney Island is 1047 on McDonald Avenue in 1954. I think that Lincoln sedan is about to pass our PCC. To the left is the Coney Island shops of the BMT Rapid Transit Division. Here all the major overhaul work is done to the subway and El fleet. The area to the left today is an expanded subway yard and at the tip, the Gil Hodges Little League field. In the past the Avenue X yard was where all of Brooklyn's trolley fleet was disposed of, until only the PCC fleet was left. This was way before the preservation of equipment was fashionable. Disposable income was not had by many and if they did have it, buying old street cars was not what would come to mind first. But some people did manage to do the impossible and save some examples.

1048

Coming down Coney Island Avenue at Park Circle 1048 encounters the rail grinder 9699 making some repairs on a stretch of track. Brooklyn had over a thousand pieces of work equipment in its time. Many former passenger cars that became old and supplanted by larger new equipment. 9699 started life as a seven window open platform single truck car. In the late 1920s it was put into work service and in the 1930s it was rebuilt into a rail grinder. It was a rare treat to see one of the big flat bed or gondola type work cars running in the streets and rarer still the rail grinder.

1049

I don't know if those ladies know it but today is the last time they will see trolleys on the 75/Smith Street line. 1049 at 15th Street and Prospect Park has only a few hours before a long history of the Smith Street line takes a drastic change to bus. It is February 10, 1951 and another line in the Brooklyn system will fall. Other lines that ceased operation in 1951 were:

Flatbush Avenue, Nostrand, Utica/Reid, Ralph/Rockaway, Holy Cross Shuttle, Rockaway Parkway, Vanderbilt, Wilson Avenue, Crosstown, Ocean and Seventh Avenue.

The City received a fleet of new Mack buses that could be converted into emergency ambulances, remember this is atomic bomb times. Within 7 years of Brooklyn streets, the Mack fleet will be falling apart.

1050

For those who require a profile shot, this is it. Turning around the back of 9th Avenue Depot is 1050. The dull paint scheme chosen by the B&QT does show off the streamline quality of the design. In many cities the blinker type doors were dropped early in favor of regular folding type doors. Chicago was a firm believer in blinker doors, they used them on their fleet and when some were converted to L cars, they kept the blinker door design. The Clark car (1000) introduced standee windows but kept the door design. If Brooklyn re-ordered a fleet of PCC cars, it is interesting to see what design changes would have been.

1051

On June 6, 1948, 1051 and 1000 are on a Triboro Fan trip. They will take their occupants on lines where the PCC will never run in revenue service. If PCC cars did operate on these lines they could have shortened schedules and increased passenger comfort. Perhaps some members still believed the City could order more PCC cars? (top left) Turning on to Myrtle Avenue from Vanderbilt the special will run under the Myrtle Avenue El. (bottom left) Here the 1051 is running on McDonald passing Greenwood Cemetery. (below right) 1051 & 1000 are at South Ferry at the foot of Atlantic Avenue. Here they meet with 8000 series cars on Fifth Avenue line at the end of its run on Atlantic Avenue and South Ferry. This area now has the Brooklyn/Queens Expressway overhead. The trip will travel to Ridgewood, over the Brooklyn Bridge and to some of the southern lines to Coney Island.

1052

1052 beating out a Plymouth at the intersection of Smith & Livingston Street. The early Brooklyn order had very interesting wind shield wipers. The pair on each window moved horizontal, right to left. In later models conventional fan shaped wipers were used. They must have been a maintenance head ache. The line is 68/Smith Street and the date is February 20, 1950. We are at the beginning of the cold war years. Television is on the move over the roofs of Brooklyn and it will have a terrible toll in downtown Brooklyn. Each one of the giant movie palaces will draw fewer and fewer movie goers. The Albee, Brooklyn Paramount and one of the Five "FABULOUS FOX" theaters will in time, disappear.

1053

It is 1946 and 1053 is on the Smith Street line. The PCC wings are history, even before the "Next Car" light. This area had a large number of factories that housed scores of various labor intense industries. Several blocks down Sands Street the great Brooklyn Navy Yard is servicing the fleet. Many trolley lines delivered workers to the navy yard from the various neighborhoods in Brooklyn. The first successful iron clad war ship, the Monitor, was built in Brooklyn Navy Yard during the Civil War. Here, it is a quiet day with light ridership and the war is now part of history.

1054

In 1950 in Brooklyn one could see a number of transportation vehicles. The St. Louis built electric bus (left) is two years in service on the Flushing Avenue line. They incorporated a light next to the front destination sign that when lighted stated "NEXT BUS" . That was a carry over from the PCC cars. I don't recall ever seeing it lighted. The trolley coaches were very quiet, clean and comfortable with large windows that opened. They were maintained at a new facility on Bergen Street and Dekalb shops in Queens. Their only problem was they were electric and not diesel powered. The subway entrance to the High Street Station of the IND 8th Avenue line. The bus (right) is one of the extra wide 4000 to 4499 GM buses that replaced most of the trolley lines. The green and silver paint schemes had variations on each vehicle.

1055

Here 1055 is a school house for training new motorman for the Brooklyn trolley system. They have one of the newest trolley cars in the nation and it operates very differently than the conventional equipment that surrounds the PCC fleet. We are outside of 9th Avenue Depot. The car will circle around the barn as each man gets his chance. A small metal sign out the front window warns passengers this is a "Instruction Car". The guys will get a new uniform if they do well. The date is June 7, 1941. However in six months on this date, everything will change, the uniform may not be that of a BMT motorman. Also there may be a few female faces looking out of the Instruction car. (bottom) 1055 coming off the Brooklyn Bridge and headed for 9th Avenue & 20th Street on the 67/Seventh Avenue line.

1056

An important junction in Brooklyn has to include Church and Flatbush Avenues. (left) Here resides the first church in Brooklyn, The Dutch Reformed Church of Flatbush. When it was built it was in the center of farms. (Top) Here in the 1950's were some of the socializing forces that made this a great area to live in. There was Garfields large cafeteria where you could get a wide variety of food or just sit and talk over coffee and rolls all day. The area had four major film houses, one of which showed foreign films. And it had the great Erasmus High School, an educational institution that has produced more important American talent than any other high school in America. 1056 has a number of passengers boarding for a trip across Church Avenue. Down Church Avenue was Jahn's Ice Cream Parlor, where you could get "The Kitchen Sink", a large ice cream sundae. There was a Macy 's and a Sears Roebuck department store. This was way before shopping centers. There were also many women's clothing stores and some very good restaurants. The Church Avenue line and Flatbush Avenue lines had heavy ridership. It was not going to Manhattan for work but, even on a Sunday, you would go for what was called, "window shopping".

1057

The BMT thought to inaugurate a special ten cents fare for a nonstop trip from downtown Brooklyn to the World's Fair in Flushing Meadows. Stopped by the City from charging a special fare the service ran only two days. However for a short time, the B&QT's new PCC could take you to see the future world. The BMT was always plagued by City Hall politics. Each mayor railed about the private traction companies getting rich by providing poor service and would never allow the raising the nickel fare, that is until the City took over ownership. Here we see 1057 on Adams Street headed for Queens in 1938 for the World's Fair dedication. (bottom) In 1950 track work was under way at Grand Army Plaza, so 1057 can only operate on the outer circle.

1058

All one can say is classy. It must be a hot day for all windows are wide open, still this is a cool trolley car. I like the BMT paint scheme. It is conservative, but I think it shows off the car's lines. But once the dirt and grime of the City gets on it, it looked terrible. The green and silver scheme was attractive and accented the cars lines very nicely. The car here is still fairly new and all new cars look great. It also looks fast even when standing still. On the Vanderbilt Avenue line at Prospect Park West in 1937. (bottom) A rear view when still new of 1058. It is at the loop at 7th Avenue and 20th Street in 1940. The trolley retriever is above the window in the "as delivered car". It will be lowered below the window, making it easier for the motorman to retrieve the trolley pole.

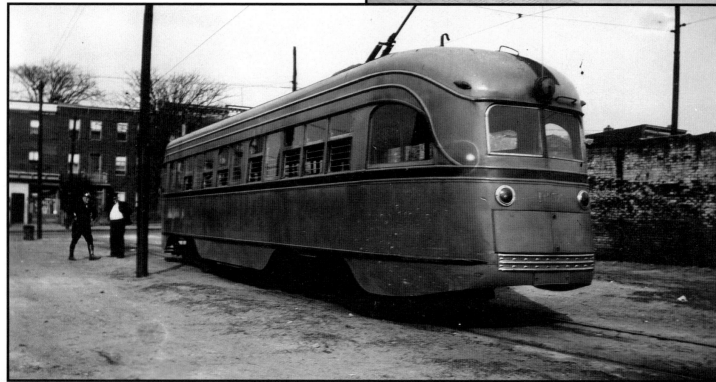

1059/1060

1059 turns in front of the south gate entrance of the Brooklyn Navy yard at Navy Street and Sands Street. It is after the storm in 1948 . The PCC was certainly functioning well while all else seems to have gone into hiding. The snow sweepers have kept the line clear. (bottom) Its October 12, 1941 and 1060 is witness to the changes for downtown Brooklyn. New trolley tracks to go down Washington street as the Fulton El. is dismantled. A whole section of the Court Street station of the Fulton El has been cut away. This was part of the urban renewal years. Adams Street will be widened to allow more traffic on and off the Brooklyn Bridge. The busy area around these structures of stores, restaurants, hotels and movie theaters will be transformed into large parks and Government office buildings, none of which pay taxes.

1061

Here 1061 moves along Flushing Avenue on the Vanderbilt Avenue route with a Flushing Avenue trolley coach in the background. Here the electric bus wire is separate from the trolley wire. The cobblestone streets do not bother the PCC. Many Brooklyn neighborhoods that struggled to keep things together during a long depression, then the War, really fell apart in peace time. The large expressways to Long Island built by Robert Moses almost emptied Brooklyn of its population. All during the 1950's, you would see friends move to Long Island. Many of the factories and manufacturing companies left for cheaper real estate and production costs. The work was gone and the workers followed. This also hit the public transit system. The Navy Yard would slowly go downhill after the War. It was a big source of riders for the Vanderbilt and Flushing lines. Soon, houses started being abandoned and areas on the fringe of busy avenues and shopping areas would show these scars. (bottom) 1061 sharing its wire with the Flushing Avenue electric coaches under the Manhattan Bridge in 1950.

1062

1061 is headed south on McDonald Avenue for Cortelyou Road and the IND subway is coming up to meet the Culver El in 1954. (bottom) A new track arrangement has trolley cars moving up Washington Street rather than Fulton Street. An 8000 and a 2500 series car are seen behind the PCC. The 2500 is running on the Bergen Street line; the 8000 could be on St Johns, Third or Dekalb lines. The El is gone and the paved over tracks will become a familiar scene as the years roll on. The year is 1941 and the Brooklyn City Hall in the background looks out on a street with no Fulton elevated rolling by. A new Twin Coach bus can be seen operating on the just converted Fulton Street trolley line.

1063

We are at the intersection of Seventh Avenue & Ninth Street in the summer of 1948. In two more years the trolley service on Smith and Seventh will be bus. The familiar clanking of a trolley rolling over the crossing will be a memory. The trolley is moving through Park Slope section of Brooklyn.

1064

We are on the Vanderbilt Avenue line at Ninth Avenue and Eighteenth Street in August 1950. It is interesting to note that both 1063 and 1064 are hitting the same things, judging by the dents in the front lower skirting. As we will see in a number of photographs, a bar in Brooklyn is only a step away. On some major avenues, there was at least one bar on every block. Thankfully Brooklyn is known as the borough of churches.

1065

The car in the top photograph is at Willoughby and Jay Streets in 1941. On the left hand corner in the early fifties will rise the new offices of the Board of Transportation, more commonly known as 370 Jay Street. This is today what is called the Metrotech area. It is only in the late 1990's that the area would get new development in the form of large office buildings and a hotel. In 2005, they are looking to tear down 370 Jay Street. (right) In 1949 we again see 1065 on Jay Street near the foot of the Manhattan Bridge. It is painted in the new scheme. The single pane, hand cranked windows gives the PCC a very open look. I also prefer the absence of standee windows in the Brooklyn fleet.

1066

In the paint shop of DeKalb car Barn, 1066 get its new colors in 1948. A 8000 series Peter Witt car is in the paint booth in the far right. The trolley car fleet of over a dozen different types all come damaged to the craftsmen of DeKalb who would rebuild the equipment as good as new. This is an era when you did not call the manufacturer for body panels or parts. The fleet ran from wood to aluminum construction. All parts were custom made by craftsmen to resemble the original even if the original was built in 1904. DeKalb had the material, machinery and talent to also build trolley cars.

1067

Here is another PCC fan trip. A few other PCC fan trips are in this book because the PCC cars moved out to other lines that they never, ever, ran in revenue service. The PCC held down daily operations on only a few lines and the reader would get tired of every picture of each car in the same area, again and again. (top) Here 1067 is at Corona Avenue on the Flushing/Ridgewood line. This line could have had PCC operation but never did, except for the 1939 Worlds Fair special service. (left) Here 1067 is seen on Grand Avenue line near the Brooklyn-Queens border. Had additional PCC's been allowed to be ordered, these two lines would have gotten PCC cars. Many of the Brooklyn lines were very long and the acceleration of the PCC would have made a significant improvement for the riders.

1068

This is a scene that is bad for the trolley and propaganda for the bus. A fire must have knocked out service on the 35/Church Avenue line and if you wanted to know how many PCC's it takes to run the service, here is your answer. The date is July 19, 1952 at E7th Street. Passengers seem to be strolling the neighborhood or waiting for service to be restored. (bottom) The police and the motorman are exchanging municipal principles of how best to get the situation resolved. This was not common, but it did occur. Rarely did it last too long. The trolley system could use temporary switches to move cars around track that was out of service (for track work) for short periods.

1069

Here at Atlantic and 4th Avenues, we see the system in transition in July 1947. 1069 is in the brand new color scheme and passes 1029 in the old B&QT colors. A St Johns Place 8000 takes the loop around the IRT's kiosk for the Atlantic Avenue. The area is dated with old institutions that are long gone from this area today, Waldorf Cafeteria and White Rose Bar. Not pictured, but not far from this spot is the Fox Movie Palace. Underneath the pavement is not only the IRT but the BMT's four track Fourth Avenue subway and Brighton Line.

1070

(right) The car is about to turn off 2nd Avenue onto 39th Street. There is now a parking lot behind it as well as parking on the streets. The year is 1953 and driving to work is more fashionable and comfortable than taking the 15 cent trolley. This area started as a large rail yard and ferry terminal but as the years go by more lots will be sold. Today a large Costco will be built where once the 39th Street shop stood. (bottom) 1070 passes 1055 on the former Culver right of way. 1055 shows the relocation of the trolley retriever to the belt line above the tail lights. The time is 1950 and the cars will have only six more years of operation. Today there is very little evidence of the rail rights of way that made Coney Island America's playground.

1071

(top) This picture shows 1071 and 1012 behind on the Canarsie Depot loop tracks. It is signed to start its trip to 39th Street Depot. In 1951 all the 6000 series single ended Peter Witt cars in the yard are going to scrap after the lines whose service they held down were abandoned to buses. To the left we can see one of them. Soon they are towed to Avenue X for scrapping. (left) 1071 shows the scars of daily service. The Dekalb Shop is no longer available to tend to its damages. 9th Street Depot is the main shop for PCC cars since 1952. The fleet has been in service for twenty years and here it rests with others on a Sunday afternoon. It will only have a few months before the curtain falls on this scene.

1072

When the Sands Street Station complex, Bridge yard, Kings County Station and the Fulton El line to Fulton Ferry were dismantled a large empty space was created. All new poles and overhead wire had to be re-strung. Here 1072 would have been under the El yard on Adams Street but today, it is in the morning light. The growth of the subway system into Brooklyn took El passengers away. The Independent 8th Avenue/Fulton line, built right under the Fulton El right of way to Queens, would eliminate the competition. The Fulton El was cut back to Rockaway Avenue. The Myrtle and Lexington Avenue El were terminated at Bridge/Jay Street station. In time, they will go too.

1073

(top) 1073 using the small loop around the Atlantic Avenue IRT kiosk to turn back. There is a disruption of service and all lines coming into downtown are being turned back. Behind a 6000 series on Flatbush is doing the same. (right) Now it is 1073's turn to disrupt downtown service. Well we have seen the dents on many of the cars, here 1073 has a big one. Its Brockway truck meets St Louis car on Washington Street . A wrecker is called to get 1073 back on track. I am sure once back on the rails it will head back to the depot and then to DeKalb shop forces. The motorman will be doing paper work for a while once back at the barn.

1074

Taps are correctly played for the last trolley to cross the Brooklyn Bridge. 1074 will do the honors bringing down the curtain on millions of trips over the famous bridge. It is March 6, 1950 at 12:09 AM. A few of the politicos of the time take the bows for this great improvement to the Brooklyn transit system. There is no evidence of the loop facility today. In fact as you look at the Brooklyn Bridge today its hard to imagine all the rail service it had. When it was built one roadway in either direction was provided for horse and wagons. Today only automobiles can cross the great bridge. (bottom) 1074 in on a Triboro Trolley Tour fan trip in 1950. It meets 1057 on the McDonald/Vanderbilt line at Grand Army Plaza. The trolley car service in Brooklyn had many private rights of way the bus would not inherit. Street car passenger islands and special cuts such as pictured below allowed the vehicle to stop and pickup passengers without stopping the auto traffic. I think that the Brooklyn PCC car always looked distinctive by having two front route and destination signs and offered flexibility for different routes. Only a few other cities had this feature.

1075

1075 is about to make a trip most of us would love to do today and just look out the window as the car went from Coney Island to Park Row Manhattan. 2583 makes a great contrast to the PCC car which is now 10 years old and is already missing its headlight wings in 1946. It is winter so the 1907 veteran 2500 will have a quiet and short trip to Sea Gate.

1076

(top) In bad weather the transit system has to be even more dependable, for the transit people have an expression for passengers who only ride public transit in snow storms or other foul weather, "Snow Birds". Here 1076 is about to turn onto 2nd Avenue and head toward Bristol Street in the winter of 1955. (left) 1076 turns out of West 5th Street Terminal on 69/McDonald/Vanderbilt headed for Park Row. A group of 2500 series cars are laying over for Sea Gate service.

1077

(top right) 1077 headed down the right toward West Fifth Street terminal with a BMT "standard" on the Culver line in 1948. (above) It's 1942 and 1077 is leaving the Sands Street station bound for the Brooklyn streets. Here they were on the same level as the El traffic. Starting in 1883 the Brooklyn Bridge Cable Railway began here; later merged in the electrified and consolidated BRT El lines.

1078

Moving over to the other side of Adams Street so that its wires don't mix with the wires from the electric bus operation, 1078 is headed for the Brooklyn Bridge. The Flushing Avenue line was converted to electric bus operation and one is coming under the Manhattan bridge. The Jehovah's Witnesses occupy a number of these factories today. This organization always restores what ever building they take over to its original look, so they have saved a small part of Brooklyn's factory architecture.

1079

Here the two photos show that 1079 had some special moments. (top) It is the inauguration of PCC service on the Erie Basin line on January 18, 1937. The ribbon is about to be cut by some of the then local Politicians. The B&QT did not have too many lines in Queens but one line that became important was the Flushing/Ridgewood line to Corona Queens. In 1938, the Corona ash pits were transformed into the greatest show that Gotham had ever produced, the 1939 World's Fair. (right) The paper sticker on 1079's dash proclaims it is a special run from the Fair to downtown Brooklyn. Here the car is on Horace Harding Boulevard with the auto traffic coming from Long Island. The B&QT presented its vision of the transportation of the future in everyday service, the PCC. This area today is lanes and lanes of highway.

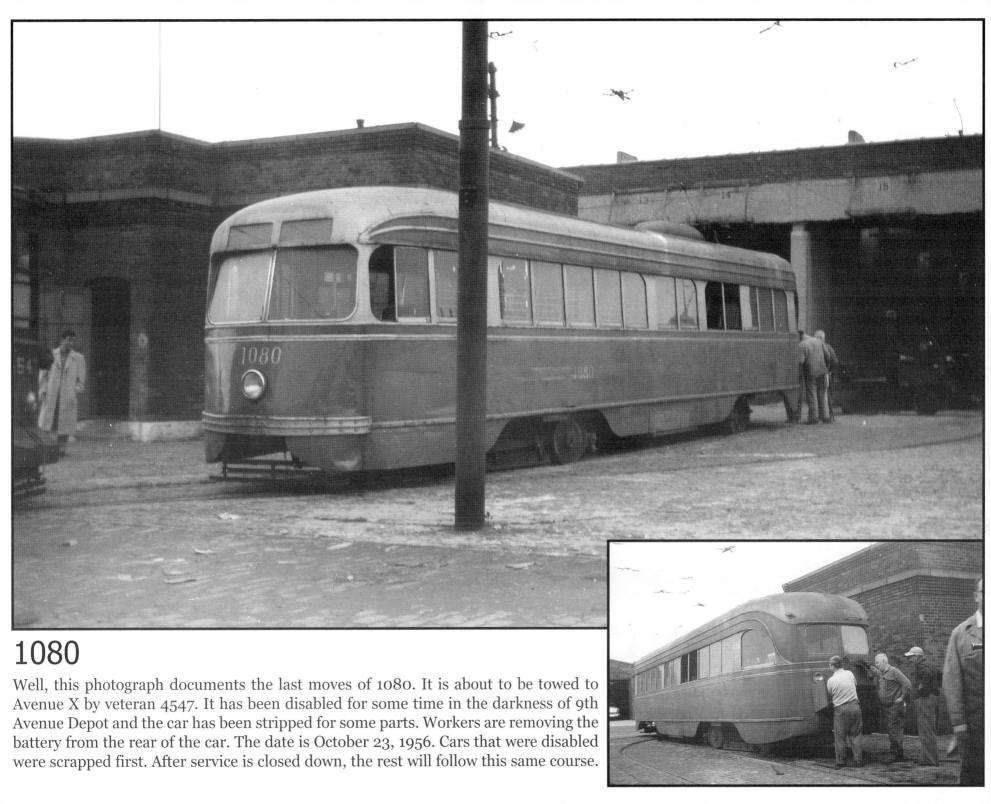

1080

Well, this photograph documents the last moves of 1080. It is about to be towed to Avenue X by veteran 4547. It has been disabled for some time in the darkness of 9th Avenue Depot and the car has been stripped for some parts. Workers are removing the battery from the rear of the car. The date is October 23, 1956. Cars that were disabled were scrapped first. After service is closed down, the rest will follow this same course.

1081

Here the trolley is about to cross the Brooklyn Bridge from the upper level of Sands Street Station. The track in the pavement was the roadway entrance to the Bridge that will merge into the track 1081 is on. 1081 has just left the Sands Street station, it was as they fashionably call today a "Multi-Modal" structure. The change for passenger's from street car to el cars on the same level was very convenient and efficient. This type of transfer was used many times in Boston but not too often in Brooklyn. The girder work over the trolley wire was an interesting feature used only at Sands street complex. A Brooklyn 8000 series is right behind.

72

1082

In 1942, 1082 waits outside DeKalb shop on special shop trucks, made from old trucks of trolley cars long gone. The War gave a life extension to some trolley lines in Brooklyn. Some lines that were replaced by buses before the War were returned again to trolley operation, like Putnam Avenue and Norton's Point line. Rubber and gasoline were vital for the War effort. (bottom) 1082 on Smith/Coney Island but signed for Hamilton Avenue means the line is being cut back. The lineup of 1035,#1016 and 1044, at the IND Smith & 9th Street Station in 1946 means there is trouble on the line. The massive subway structure dwafts this little industrial area. The car has been in service for a decade and looks as good as new.

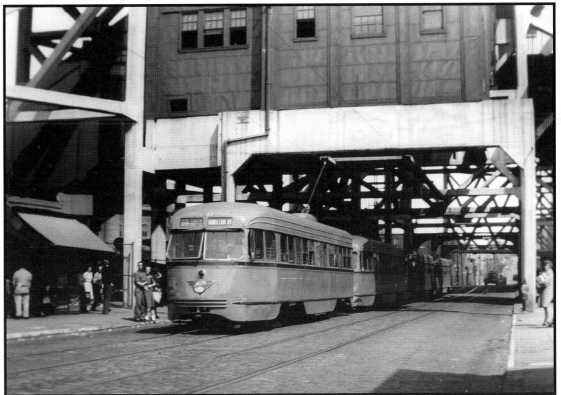

1083

Under the Culver El at Avenue X, 1083 moves with an Oldsmobile of the period down McDonald Avenue. It may be the writer's view but the PCC design looks more modern and elegant than the automobile: designed years after the PCC. The PCC design is a true test of art, it holds up years after its introduction. To the left out of this photograph is the beginning of the BMT Coney Island shop complex. The South Brooklyn Railroad will at this time still deliver new subway cars from the Long Island Railroad or railroad car floats to Coney Island shops via McDonald Avenue.

1084

(left) Crossing Coney Island Avenue while on Church in 1954. This was a favorite corner for the great Brooklyn trolley historian Edward B. Watson. Behind the car we see another type of Architecture, walkup row houses, that are typical of Brooklyn and Queens. The year is the summer of 1954 and probably on a summer Sunday. The Church Avenue line was a slow west to east line. The PCC did their best to speed up the service but auto traffic and local deliveries would make that job difficult. In a few blocks, it will duck under Ocean Parkway on its way to First Avenue.

1085/1086

Here we see 1085 in Summer 1950 about to enter the Grand Army Plaza by Prospect Park. The large Brooklyn park is our back drop for both photographs. Street parking is more available in this 1950 view; not everyone owned a car yet. The car is on the Vanderbilt Avenue line and will head toward 20th Street. Here next to the park it may be a little cooler than the tree-less streets elsewhere on its route. (left) A rear view at Bartel Pritchard Square and we can see the illuminated "STOP" lights. This idea was taken from the automobile and very useful to cars that followed the trolley. The two rear panel doors hide the PCC battery box. They don't have that smooth contoured look it had when the car was new. The Vanderbilt line just skirts the west side of the park. Only the Flatbush Avenue line went through the park.

1087

(top) Looking bright in the Brooklyn sunlight 1088 heads to Coney Island. The car will make that distinct PCC noise when making this turn onto McDonald Avenue. It is the fall of 1948. (right) 1087 turns onto Myrtle Avenue. The large ugly walkway connects to the Bridge/Jay Street station. The El to Park Row from here is gone and in time so will Myrtle the Avenue El. Myrtle Avenue, where the trolley is pictured turning, will disappear. An underground municipal parking facility is to be built where the street and business establishments and movie theaters were. Today instead of a parking garage, a new hotel occupies this spot.

1088

(right) 1088 is at Adams and Sands Street. The PCC came at the right time to handle the additional ridership made possible by the war effort. The war brought many Brooklynites back on the job. Defense-related industries were everywhere, especially along the factories that ran from 58th Street in Bay Ridge to Greenpoint. The Naval Tailors so near the navy yard must have been a busy place. The passengers can board a trolley without fear of being mowed down, but this is 1944. The car at the end of the line on High Street at the Brooklyn Bridge. (below) It is time to take a mechanical look at 1088 at Dekalb shop. There is a rather long scrape along the side of the car. DeKalb was enlarged in 1927 to be the main shop of the trolley fleet. It repaired every variety of Brooklyn trolley. Today it is an athletic field for Junior High School 162.

1089

(top) Its May 25, 1941 and the main stay of the Brooklyn fleet assembled according to age. The 8000, to 6000 to the new PCC cars. Here under the Fulton El passengers gather to get the right line. Under ground the original IRT & BMT subways also run. The history of Brooklyn's transportation is a history of its population growth, from small Dutch farms to the fourth largest city in America. (left) Moving along Church Avenue at E18th Street in 1954 heading toward First Avenue. The architecture behind can be found in this neighborhood and in other areas around the borough. A Brooklynite can tell were they are by the Architecture indicative to that neighborhood. Most areas were settled by one large developer who produced the same style, over and over again. Living on a busy Avenue has an advantage; you don't have to get in a car to get the paper, milk or fresh morning bagels.

1090

(top) Here at Jay and Tillary Streets in 1937, we can see how well the design of the PCC fit into the Brooklyn landscape. The windows open and elbows sticking out, only on the one side of the car was this possible. The other side had chrome window bars on the inside of the windows, in time they would be put in all windows. This was because of the close clearance between passing cars. These modern window bars were installed on some 8000 series Peter Witt cars. This whole area is very different today but not as pleasant as in this photo.

1091/1092

(top) Coming down Sands Street and about to turn on Vanderbilt Avenue on the McDonald/Vanderbilt line in 1949. The run down area is near the Navy yard and is lightly populated. The Flushing Avenue electric bus wires are overhead. (left) At the open space between barns inside 9th Avenue & 20th Street car barn, 4573, a work motor, is on the left in the shadows. It is 1948 and for its short career on the streets 1092 looks the worse for wear over 4573 I'll bet. The 4500 were bigger, higher cars with large steel bumpers and steel side sills. They as work motors do not have to go out on the line every day.

1093

(top) Another shot from the Fulton El of the trolley activity on Court Street. A 4100 to the left is about to turn on Court and down the street is a steady stream of 8000, 4100 and PCC type cars. It is a clear day in 1937. 1093 is running on Erie Basin line. (left) Another view of 1093 is in an area most people never saw. The transfer table in 9th Avenue & 20th Street car barn serviced the area used for maintenance work. Here lesser class repairs were made. In these narrow stalls, not well lit and certainly open to the elements, the craftsmen kept the fleet in top shape. The BMT and the surface B&QT made a big effort in being able to maintain and rebuild their Trolley, El and subway equipment. The shop forces were the heart of the company.

1094

(top) Here in April 1938 we see the company's attempt to earn new cash by providing extra fare (10 cents) service for a direct trip from downtown Brooklyn to the World's Fair site in Flushing Meadow, Queens. The city administration soon put a stop to the service while at the same time charging 10 cents to ride its IND line to the Fair and 15 cents for a direct bus line. Judging from the line at Myrtle near Washington Street into 1094, the ridership would have been good and convenient to the public. (right) Sitting on the Park Row loop with a 6000 type and a shelter car to the right. The shelter car was a former convertible passenger car, 3740, which was used as a waiting room.

1095

Framed by a factory the Bush Terminal complex meant lots of fares on the week day but on week ends it could be a lonely world. 1095 turns off 2nd Avenue onto private right of way to double loop terminal. The ferry service is long gone. This area still hosts a number of factories that make all sorts of items today. The New York metropolitan area is a large consumer of all kinds of goods and clothing and it is still possible that some items are made in Brooklyn.

1096

For many years, passengers transferred to the McDonald trolley to go to Coney Island. The Brooklyn trolley system had a great transfer system where for one fare you could change to another line and keep riding. As a child, my mother only went to Coney Island by trolley. If you lived in the Bushwick section, it was faster than taking the subway. The subway lines ran into Manhattan, then transfer for the southern division BMT to Coney Island. On a Sunday we would take the DeKalb bus (post 1949), transfer to the Vanderbilt trolley, and change (where this photo is taken), to the McDonald car. In this 1953 picture we are right in front of the 9th Avenue & 20th Street barn and some stalls at this end no longer had tracks and were used for trucks or employee parking. Boarding a car and going around the barn at the other end one could see other types of equipment stored in the dark interiors. As a kid and a trolley fan, it was a great experience.

1097

A new 1097 coming down 9th street at 2nd Avenue in 1936 in Smith Street service. The route goes through a busy neighborhood and industrial areas in Brooklyn. The second overhead wire lead to the Roulston grocery warehouse when Brooklyn ran trolley freight. The Depression slowed many of the factories along the line and passenger ridership dropped. The economic and attractive qualities of the PCC helped to lift ridership on this and other lines on which it ran. (bottom) Here in its new paint scheme it is next to the present new vehicle in service, the electric bus on St. John's Place route. The PCC design looks fresher compared to the boxy electric bus, although they were built in the same place and share a common manufacturer.

1098

Our car is on the top of the Coney Island Avenue bridge over the Belt Parkway in 1955. This is one of the few areas where double arm trolley poles were used on the system; it was not common on the B&QT. The new bridge had to use a new pole design. By now the sea of black derby filial on the poles were no longer available. This type of track laid in concrete made for a smoother and quieter ride. It made the PCC seem as if it was gliding on air.

1099

Here are views in both the good times and bad. Left we see 1099 in special World's Fair service under the Fulton El in 1938. The right side, the last PCC at the final hour in Coney Island shop complex, where most of the remaining fleet of cars were picked up by the scrap dealer. Many would stay sitting at the scrap dealer for a few more years, until the yard itself was abandoned. Through it all, 1099 managed to retain its PCC headlamp wings while other cars had shed them along the way. The Brooklyn PCC pioneered and proved the value of this streamline trolley and that will last forever.